Contents

1. PREHISTORY: *Skin on skin. But first...they had to catch it.*   4-7
2. ANCIENT EGYPT: *Elegance & nobility on the banks of the Nile*   8-11
3. ANCIENT GREECE: *Beauty of body & soul*   12-13
4. ANCIENT ROME: *Metres and metres of coloured fabric*   14-15
5. CELTS: *Hurray for breeches!*   16-17
6. CHINA: *Land of the dragon & silk*   18-19
7. JAPAN: *The immortal kimono*   20-21
8. INDIA: *The flowing sari & the original pyjamas*   22-23
9. THE MIDDLE AGES: *Knights & princesses*   24-27
10. TUDORS: *Slim waists & rounded bellies*   28-29
11. 17TH CENTURY: *Rounded silhouettes*   30-33
12. COURT CLOTHES: *Flowers, gold & ornament*   34-35
13. EMPIRE INSPIRED: *A fashion revolution in soft colours*   36-37
14. ROMANTICISM: *Haute couture & wasp waists*   38-39
15. EDWARDIAN ERA: *The travel 'bug' & innovative machines*   40-43
16. ART NOUVEAU: *Colours & shapes inspired by nature*   44-47
17. THE ROARING 20S: *Dance fashion with a jazz rhythm*   48-49
18. THE FORTIES: *Improvise & economise*   50-51
19. THE FIFTIES: *A fashion for billowing skirts*   52-55
20. THE SIXTIES: *Flower power & moonwalks*   56-59
21. THE SEVENTIES: *Disco fever!*   60-61
22. THE EIGHTIES: *Plastic mania*   62-63
23. THE NINETIES: *London style!*   64-65
24. CONTEMPORARY FASHION: *Unique choices*   66-67

TIMELINES

Around the fashion world   68-71
Fashion icons   72
Swimwear   73
Ladies' hats   74
Hairstyles   74
Wedding dresses   75
Fashion designers & their creations   76-77
Handbags & shoes   78

Glossary   79
Index   80

Don't be scared – it's only Dad!

SKIN ON SKIN.
But first...they had to catch it.

Imagine what it must have been like for people in prehistoric times. They lived in cold caves or simple shelters made from wood, straw and mud, or anything they could lay their hands on. They had no shops, and no one yet knew how to make cloth. So what did they wear to keep warm? They wore fur! Prehistoric people wrapped themselves in animal skins, fastened together with pins made of bone.

Look – another dumb mammoth!

NEW!

The latest gadget every woman wants – a bone needle!

First needle

A few thousand years later someone invented the first needle! By making a small hole in a bone pin, and threading it with a blade of grass (or animal sinew), it could be used to stitch clothing together.

HELPFUL HINTS:
HOW TO MAKE A FUR COAT

First stretch out the animal skin in the sun to dry. Then rub animal fat into the skin and knead it until it is soft and pliable. Stitch the skins together to make a garment that lasts for generations.

HORSETAIL FURS
Hunt your own outfit!

1 +1 mammoth
FREE

Prehistoric clothing could be surprisingly useful. Hunters wore deer skins as a disguise to get closer to their prey without scaring it away.

The skins of tigers, leopards and bears were thought to have special powers that brought success in the next hunt. They were highly prized and only the bravest hunters and most important tribe members could wear them.

DRESS YOUR WHOLE TRIBE!
1 MAMMOTH MAKES 25 GARMENTS

Venus!

THE PERFECT ADORNMENT FOR EVERY HOUSEHOLD

The ideal prehistoric woman is anything but skinny. In fact, Venus figurines usually portrayed very buxom, motherly females.

THE FIRST LOOM

Bronze and Iron Ages

As the Earth warmed up, people stopped moving on in search of food. They domesticated animals, and learned to spin thread from flax or sheep's wool, and to weave fabrics on simple looms. They discovered bronze and iron, which they cast and forged into magnificent jewellery.

HELPFUL HINTS:
HOW TO BECOME A WEAVER

Stick two branches in the ground and lay a third branch across the top. Congratulations, you have just built a loom! Now tie lots of yarns to the top branch, then tie stones or clay weights to the other ends. These are the warp threads. The weft threads are now woven horizontally in and out of the warp threads. Keep weaving until you have made a length of cloth.

FIRST DOMESTICATED ANIMALS

PREHISTORIC MAN'S BEST FRIEND?

FIRST DOMESTICATED DOG

A VISIT TO THE PREHISTORIC JEWELLERS

Perforated tooth necklace
Middle Stone Age
(100,000 BC)

Snail shell beads
Later Stone Age
(10,000 BC)

Stone beads
Early Bronze Age
(2000 BC)

Bronze necklace
Middle Bronze Age
(1500 BC)

Wrought gold bracelet
Middle Bronze Age
(1400 BC)

Wrought gold collar
Later Bronze Age
(800 BC)

Simple bronze brooch
Earlier Iron Age
(600 BC)

Gold earrings and necklace
Earlier Iron Age
(500 BC)

Gold collar and earrings
Later Iron Age
(300 BC)

ROMANTIC GIFT FOR VALENTINE'S DAY:
A necklace made of perforated teeth

It took great skill to drill through a hard tooth or a shell using a small bow-drill: a stick with a sharp flint tip. This was rotated to make a hole. They later went on to make beads by drilling holes in various materials. Just a few centuries later they learned to smelt and shape gleaming metals.

Ancient Egypt

3150 – 30 BC

FAN MADE OF BIRD FEATHERS

WIG

GOLDEN COBRA

FALSE BEARD

CROOK

FLAIL

PERSONAL SANDAL CARRIER

My latest model – sandals made from reeds.

Lack of respect a problem? Get yourself **A BEARD!**

ELEGANCE & NOBILITY ON THE BANKS OF THE NILE

Ancient Egypt is the birthplace of fashion. Clothes were worn for beauty, not warmth. For official occasions, the pharaoh, Egypt's ruler, wore a tunic with an embroidered hem. The pharaoh's crown, royal crook and flail symbolised his power. The royal beard inspired respect, so pharoahs wore fake beards made of metal – some queens did, too! Egyptian women wore translucent, pleated robes made from the finest cotton or linen. These garments were worn with gold collars inlaid with blue, green and red semi-precious stones.

CROWNS FOR EVERY OCCASION!

Protective vulture crown **1**.

A blue crown **2** was worn when fighting and hunting. It was decorated with a golden cobra to frighten the pharaoh's enemies.

A feather crown **3** made from two long ostrich feathers.

A crown combining the white headdress of Upper Egypt and the red headdress of Lower Egypt **4** . The white symbolises Upper Egypt, and the red Lower Egypt.

Eye-shadow for Beauty?

Did you know that the Ancient Egyptians wore eye-shadow? It protected their eyelids from the hot Saharan sun – a bit like wearing sunglasses. The Egyptians emphasised their eyes by outlining them with black powder called kohl. Kohl contains poisonous lead which was thought to protect the eyes from diseases, but it certainly didn't do their health any good…

"Guess who inspired that eyeliner look?"

When a pharaoh dies, his clothes and jewels go with him to his tomb. But before his royal burial, his body must be mummified to preserve it. It is dried in a salt solution before being stuffed and embalmed with fragrant oils and ointments. The body is then wrapped in thin strips of resin-soaked linen bandages.

I want my own clothes back... these bandages are uncomfortable!

Cleopatra and Nefertiti

Cleopatra, a famous Egyptian queen, used honey face masks for her complexion. Two Roman emperors – Caesar and Mark Anthony – both fell in love with her. However, it was Queen Nefertiti who was thought to be the most beautiful woman in the ancient world. The name, Nefertiti, means "the beautiful one has arrived".

Early perfumes

For celebrations, ladies' wigs were topped with a perfumed cone of fat. The cone released a pleasant fragrance as it melted in the heat.

Magical Jewels

Young children wore no clothes and their heads were shaved. Only one lock of hair was left to grow and it was cut off on the day they reached adulthood. Jewellery or amulets with a scarab beetle, an Ankh cross, or the eye of the god Horus were supposed to drive away evil spirits. Rich girl's dresses were decorated with beaded netting for any celebrations. Poorer girls had to make do with a beaded waistband.

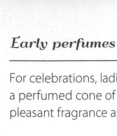

BRACELET WITH SCARAB

PLEATED TUNIC

EYE OF THE GOD HORUS

PERFUMED CONE

ANKH CROSS

BEADED NETTING

WIG

Mmm... you smell nice. Mummy no.5?

Hey, Mum, is that Cleopatra?

Is that bread not ready yet?

Come back in an hour.

Men's fashion trends

Tunic made with fringed plants

Fabric loin-cloth

Common People

Ordinary people wore simpler clothing without any decoration and most walked barefoot. Richer Egyptians wore sandals made from palm leaves, reeds or papyrus. Butchers also wore sandals to avoid walking barefoot through pools of blood on the floor.

Peasant

Baker

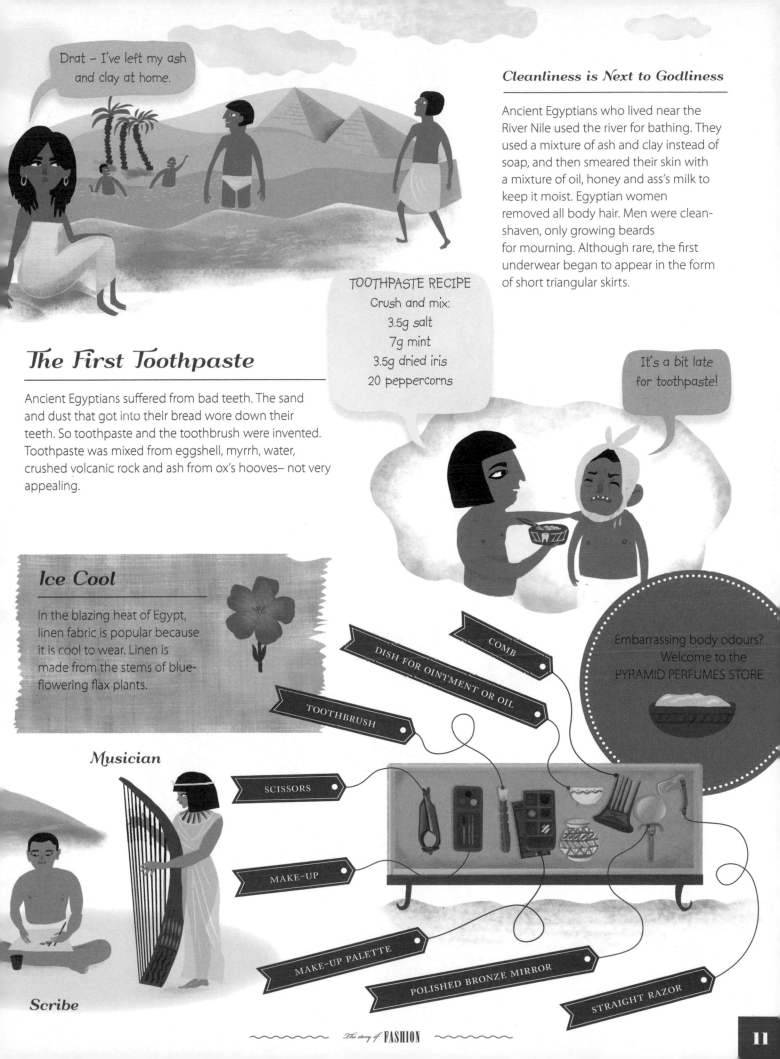

Drat – I've left my ash and clay at home.

Cleanliness is Next to Godliness

Ancient Egyptians who lived near the River Nile used the river for bathing. They used a mixture of ash and clay instead of soap, and then smeared their skin with a mixture of oil, honey and ass's milk to keep it moist. Egyptian women removed all body hair. Men were clean-shaven, only growing beards for mourning. Although rare, the first underwear began to appear in the form of short triangular skirts.

TOOTHPASTE RECIPE
Crush and mix:
3.5g salt
7g mint
3.5g dried iris
20 peppercorns

The First Toothpaste

Ancient Egyptians suffered from bad teeth. The sand and dust that got into their bread wore down their teeth. So toothpaste and the toothbrush were invented. Toothpaste was mixed from eggshell, myrrh, water, crushed volcanic rock and ash from ox's hooves– not very appealing.

It's a bit late for toothpaste!

Ice Cool

In the blazing heat of Egypt, linen fabric is popular because it is cool to wear. Linen is made from the stems of blue-flowering flax plants.

Embarrassing body odours? Welcome to the PYRAMID PERFUMES STORE

COMB

DISH FOR OINTMENT OR OIL

TOOTHBRUSH

Musician

SCISSORS

MAKE-UP

MAKE-UP PALETTE

POLISHED BRONZE MIRROR

STRAIGHT RAZOR

Scribe

03 Ancient Greece

800 – 30 BC

BEAUTY OF BODY & SOUL

The ancient Greeks are famous for their wisdom and learning, but also for their love of bathing, sport and health. Their clothes were simple and elegant. They wore wide tunics, **1** hitched up into folds and belted at the waist. They also wore lightweight garments called chitons **2** or a peplos, a warmer woollen version. A himation was a cloak that looked like a blanket wrapped around the body. **3** In bad weather, women would draw it up over their hair. Soldiers and hunters wore a short cloak, fastened at the shoulder, called a chlamys. Wide-brimmed hats were sometimes worn, too.

The sign of a modern man
A SMOOTH-SHAVEN FACE

Sport

Boys took part in sport from an early age. They ran and competed in the long jump and throwing the javelin and discus. Athletes at the Olympic Games usually competed naked, their oiled bodies gleaming in the sunshine. Girls were not allowed to participate in the games.

Warriors & Whiskers

In early adulthood, the ancient Greeks cut their hair and sacrificed it to the gods. They took pride in keeping their hair short. Alexander the Great advised his soldiers to shave off their beards so that the enemy could not grab hold of them while fighting.

Spas

The ancient Greeks enjoyed bathing several times a day. A quick bath in the morning and a more thorough one later in the day.

4

 HELPFUL HINTS: **HOW TO PUT ON A CHITON**

1.

You need a large rectangular piece of material and two decorated clasps. Now take hold of the material with both hands as though you were drying your back with it.

2.

Use one hand to bring a section of the material forward across your body and towards your shoulder. Fasten it with a clasp. Be careful to fasten sufficient material and not just the corner edge.

3.

Now fasten the material at the front and back of your other shoulder with a second clasp.

4.

Tie a cord or thin belt around your waist to complete your chiton.

Ancient Rome

27 BC – 476 AD

I will captivate her with my knowledge!

Hm, we'll see... Wait till she sees my new toga!

Greek

Roman

On top & underneath

The Roman toga ❶ was an oval piece of fabric almost the length of a fully grown tree! Underneath it they wore a tunic which was wound around the body several times. ❷ In cold weather two tunics might be worn or even four, if it was really cold. Women wore a palla draped over a tunic ❸ or a lightweight dress known as a stola. ❹ Cloaks were fastened at the shoulder with a clasp called a fibula. ❺ Children wore protective amulets around their necks. ❻

METRES AND METRES OF COLOURED FABRIC

The Romans took their inspiration from Greek fashion, but they thought it was a little too serious and boring. So, they decided to add their own special touches: a few extra metres of fabric, some more colour and interesting borders. Lo and behold, Roman attire was suddenly much richer and grander!

Tyrian Purple

Purple was a highly prized colour which was extracted from sea snails. The process was lengthy, complicated and expensive. Only emperors and senators were allowed to wear purple.

LAUNDRY

The Romans did not use soap. They massaged oils into their skin and then scraped it off along with any dirt. You think that's strange? Laundry was cleaned with sulphur or urine!

A 'MUST HAVE' CLASSIC FOR YOUR SHOE COLLECTION!

Get yourself some **GLADIATOR SANDALS!**

Roman emperors wore wreaths made of laurel or bay leaves on their heads. For Romans the laurel symbolised glory and victory, and was also supposed to protect against disaster.

CURLING IRONS
Curl your hair with red-hot irons to create ringlets.

Use a false hairpiece for those 'big hair' creations!

Jewellery

Sea corals, pearls and amber were fashionable stones. Men and women both wore rings which were often given as a token of friendship or love, or exchanged by a bride and groom. Noblemen also used rings as seals for business deals. Generally only one ring was worn, however, those who wanted to show off their wealth might wear as many as ten!

900 – 12 BC

FUR

HOODED CLOAK

BROOCH

A brooch made of iron, bronze, silver or gold.

STRIPS OF CLOTH

Strips of cloth were wound around the calves for warmth.

WOOLLEN SOCKS

BREECHES

POUCH WITH COMB

HURRAY FOR BREECHES!

As far as the Greeks and Romans were concerned, anyone who spoke a different language was a barbarian. But they had to concede that these primitive and crude barbarians, the Celts, did have some clever ideas – breeches, for instance! Hard as they tried to resist them, comfort soon won out. Roman soldiers were the first to wear breeches, which looked like two tubes stitched together. The Celts came up with the idea of long sleeves, too, which came in handy in winter.

The northern tribes wore practical clothing that was suitable for all weathers. They always carried a pouch with a comb in it to take care of their long hair and beards.

ADVERTISEMENT

A GIFT OF RECONCILIATION?
Soap made from chestnut kernels

CELTS & ROMANS: TUNIC VS TROUSERS

Roman: What strange gear these Celts wear!

Celt: Better than wearing a skirt!

Roman: You'd be glad of a skirt now, wouldn't you?

Ok between us now?

Socks

The Ancient Egyptians wore socks, **1** but it was the Celts who initiated a real boom in sock-wearing. Coming from harsh, cold climates, they swore by their warm socks **2** , which they wore inside knitted boots **3** . The Romans picked up the sock habit from the Celts, and wore socks with their sandals **4** !

Soap

Greeks and Romans had something else to thank the Celts for. The discovery of **soap** meant that they no longer had to oil and scrape their bodies to keep clean.

Dyes

The Celts looked fearsome going into battle. They painted their bodies with blue dye and wore fur, and bright-coloured clothing. They made dyes from plants and berries. The women used red berries to paint their nails. Unpainted nails were a social disgrace.

Celts

Wandering poets, musicians and storytellers were given bracelets as gifts.

Women and men wore plaited neck rings.

If a Celtic man committed a crime his beard was shaved off and he had to forfeit rights, such as his right to vote. These rights were restored once his beard had grown back.

LAND OF THE DRAGON & SILK

The Silk Road was an overland network of trade routes that linked the East to the West. Getting to Asia took many months. Chinese fashions, therefore, evolved in isolation, giving rise to quite different garments and materials from those in Europe. The Chinese had always dressed in silk but they carefully guarded the secret of how it was made. Traders thronged the Silk Road, seeking these fine fabrics which were unrivalled in their beauty. The secret behind the fine threads of silk was finally revealed when two monks smuggled the cocoons of silkworm moths to Europe in their hollow bamboo staves.

PEACOCK FEATHER

Speak up, will you!!! What did you say?

The emperor awarded a peacock feather for services rendered.

EMPE...

Silkworm

Silk cocoon

Throw away that spindle and distaff – get yourself

A SPINNING WHEEL!

Spindle and Distaff ✗   The spinning wheel ✓

Knots

Knotwork jewellery and decorations are traditional in China. Each knotted shape contains information: large knots stand for important events and small knots for everyday ones.

The special hats worn by officials were supposed to prevent them getting close enough to whisper and influence each other during court proceedings. The emperor had to make his announcements loud and clear.

HAT

What???

OFFICIAL

Hanfu

The traditional Chinese garment made of silk satin is called hanfu, and is made up of many layers. It was embroidered with flowers, animals, mountains and lakes to symbolise the eternal harmony of people and nature. Soldiers' clothing might feature wild animals like tigers and bears, while an official's rank could be recognised by the bird embroidered on his chest. The emperor's clothing was embroidered with gold dragons because he represented "the dragon who fell from heaven".

Foot binding

Chinese girls had their feet bound to restrict their growth in order to wear tiny shoes in adulthood. The ideal foot length was 7cm. Their chronically deformed feet made walking difficult and very painful. This practice was outlawed in 1902 by the empress Cixi.

STRAW HAT

SHOES MADE OF BAMBOO

Ordinary people wore fabrics made of hemp.

220 – 589

420 – 589

618 – 907

960 – 1279

1368 – 1644

1644 – 1911

1911 – 1920

1930 – 1940

1940 – 1960

21ST CENTURY

THE IMMORTAL KIMONO

The traditional Japanese kimono was worn by geisha and samurai for thousands of years. It has undergone many changes but still survives to this day. In ancient times girls were chosen from an early age to become geisha. They learned calligraphy and origami, how to play a musical instrument, flower-arranging or the art of serving tea at a tea ceremony. A geisha's role was to keep men company. They had to dance, sing or entertain them with poetry or conversation.

GEISHA

OBI BELT

The Geisha Look

Whiten your face by applying a paste made of white rice powder. Pluck out your eyebrows and paint them back on in red and black. Paint your eyelids, too. Add a tiny touch of bright carmine red to your lips. A painted comb and decorated hairpins will complete your hairstyle.

Flip-flops: Made in Japan

Today's flip-flop sandals originate from those traditionally worn by geisha. They wore special socks called tabi with them. Tabi have a gap between the toes for the sandal strap.

HAKOSEKO

This practical purse tucks into the neckline of your kimono.

Do you prefer noisy shoes… or quiet ones?

Wooden geta

Straw waraji

CHERRY BLOSSOM

SAMURAI IN EVERYDAY CLOTHES

SAMURAI IN BATTLE GEAR

KATANA

NOH

KYOGEN

In the Heian period, women's kimonos consisted of up to 20 different layers of co-ordinated colours. A beautiful woman must wear her hair long and loose, redden her lips – and blacken her teeth!

Wealthy diamyo lords and landowners wore wide sleeved garments. These often had five emblems on the shoulders, sleeves and back to indicate the wearer's social class or family. By contrast, sumo wrestlers wore nothing but a loincloth when competing in the arena!

Sumo wrestlers

Japanese rulers were served by warriors called samurai. They wore armour made of hardwood and rawhide, and carried a special sword called a katana.

Let's go to the theatre!

If you prefer serious performances, try noh. If it's fun you want, go for kyogen. Both use traditional masks to depict the actor's role, age and his character's mood.

This is not football, but kemari! Players did not compete, but worked together to keep the ball in the air for as long as possible. This was difficult with such long-sleeved clothing!

In ancient times, men and women's clothing consisted of a loose shirt and even looser trousers or skirt, often belted with some fabric. They wore their hair in chignons or pigtails.

THE FLOWING SARI & THE ORIGINAL PYJAMAS

A traditional Indian sari is worn by women. It is a long strip of material wrapped around the body, with one end draped over the shoulder or over the head like a veil. Under the sari, women wear a short blouse that reveals the navel. The sari is still worn today, and for celebratory occasions such as weddings and birthdays. A wedding sari is a richly decorated garment.

BINDI

HALF-SARI

SARI

HENNA TATTOO

CASHMERE SHAWL

Cotton boll

In addition to saris, women have also worn half-saris. These are made up of three pieces– a long skirt, a top and a shawl. The shawl is tucked into the edge of the skirt and then draped over the shoulder.

BE HEALTHY – WEAR JEWELLERY!

According to Indian tradition, jewellery purifies. This is why women wear a lot of gold bracelets and a gold ring in their nose.

Batik

Beautifully soft cashmere shawls are made from the wool of the cashmere goat. The material is printed or dyed. When fabric is tie-dyed, a design is created by string or by drawing with hot wax. It is then placed in dye. Areas tied with string or painted with wax remain undyed, forming wonderful patterns.

Cashmere pattern

DYER

WOODEN PRINTING BLOCK

TURBAN

ORIENTAL SLIPPERS

KURTA SHIRI

A little bit of India in every bedroom

Guess which piece of clothing developed from the Indian tunic and trousers? Yes, pyjamas!

Ancient Indians clothed themselves very simply. Woven fabric was just wrapped around the body. Men wound the cotton fabric around and then passed it between their legs to make dhoti trousers: a garment halfway between a skirt and trousers.

💡 HELPFUL HINTS: **THE TURBAN STEP BY STEP**

1. 2. 3.
4. 5. 6.

DHOTI

TIE-DYE BATIK

WAX BATIK

PRINTER

Cashmere goat

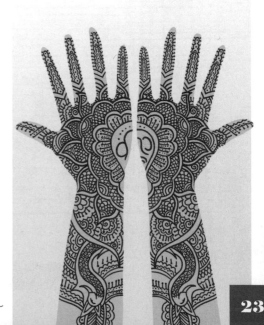

The Middle Ages

500 – 1500 AD

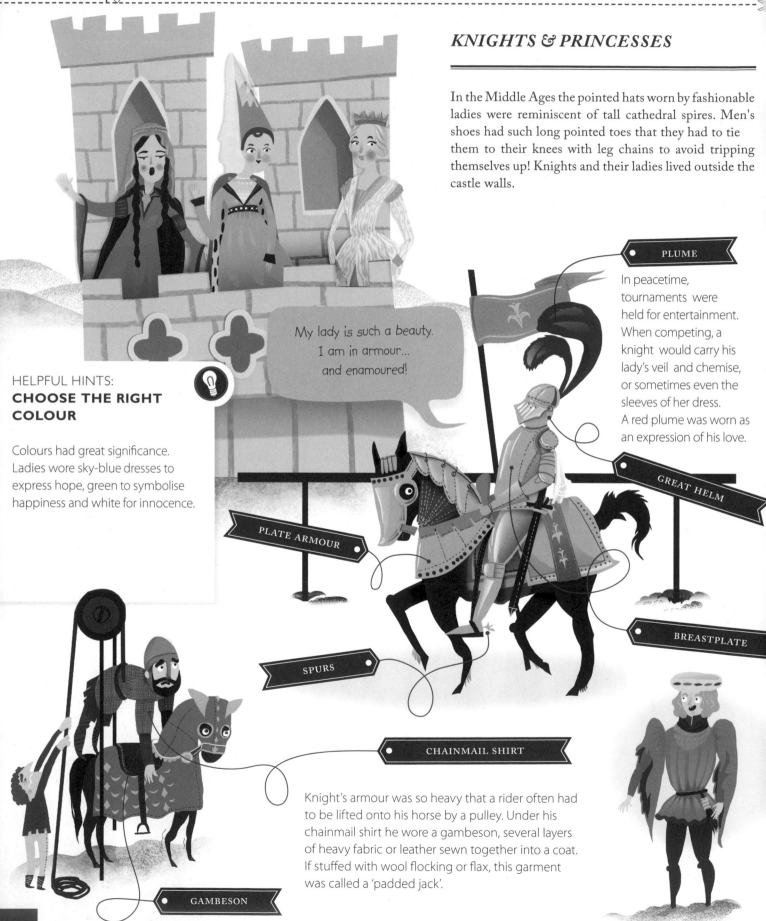

KNIGHTS & PRINCESSES

In the Middle Ages the pointed hats worn by fashionable ladies were reminiscent of tall cathedral spires. Men's shoes had such long pointed toes that they had to tie them to their knees with leg chains to avoid tripping themselves up! Knights and their ladies lived outside the castle walls.

My lady is such a beauty.
I am in armour...
and enamoured!

HELPFUL HINTS:
CHOOSE THE RIGHT COLOUR

Colours had great significance. Ladies wore sky-blue dresses to express hope, green to symbolise happiness and white for innocence.

PLUME

In peacetime, tournaments were held for entertainment. When competing, a knight would carry his lady's veil and chemise, or sometimes even the sleeves of her dress. A red plume was worn as an expression of his love.

GREAT HELM

PLATE ARMOUR

BREASTPLATE

SPURS

CHAINMAIL SHIRT

Knight's armour was so heavy that a rider often had to be lifted onto his horse by a pulley. Under his chainmail shirt he wore a gambeson, several layers of heavy fabric or leather sewn together into a coat. If stuffed with wool flocking or flax, this garment was called a 'padded jack'.

GAMBESON

The Catholic Church disapproved of too many buttons, tight lacing, low necklines and the provocative sight of a lady's bare ankle. In fact, they disapproved of almost everything!

Hi! Guess where I got these fabrics from?

LONG SLEEVES WITH TIPPETS

COLOURED TIGHTS

The rich used colour to distinguish themselves from the poor who had to make do with dull shades of brown and grey. Few people dared to walk barefoot as all manner of waste was poured directly into the streets. Stockings were generally worn by men, ideally with a different colour for each leg!

All Fools' Day

On All Fools' Day poor people were allowed to dress up like the rich and to make fun of them. Otherwise a strict dress code applied; those who flouted it could be locked up or driven out of town.

BELL SLEEVES

Drat, I was in a hurry to get out!

Wearing the same coloured stockings?

LEG CHAINS FOR SHOES

'MUST-HAVES' FOR YOUR BELT

Pockets had not been invented so pouches, purses and wallets were carried instead. ❶ A lady would hang a small bottle of scent on her belt ❷ or a posy of fragrant flowers. Men always carried a sword or a dagger. ❸

LONG, POINTED SHOES

- Do not paint your face.
- For a fine complexion, wash in early morning dew or rosewater.
- Apply beaten eggs to your face to remedy a tired appearance.
- Ask your herbalist for some beeswax lipbalm, and some chamomile extract for your hair.

STARCHED LINEN BONNET

METAL CIRCLET

CRESPINE

Hair – the crowning glory

The medieval ideal of beauty comprised of flowing locks, a high forehead and a snow-white complexion. Young women wore their hair long and loose or in braids with a floral garland, a circlet, a crespine or a bonnet. A married woman's hair was covered with a cap and veil. Pale skin was a sign of a high-born girl who did not have to toil in the fields in all weathers. Women who wore make-up were considered vain and sinful.

. . . the winners of the medieval beauty pageant are . . . Goldilocks for her golden hair, Snow White for her snow-white skin and Sleeping Beauty for her rosy cheeks!

Red, blue or green?

Were Medieval people grubby?

Some were cleaner than others. Even the most stubborn sometimes splashed themselves with water. Some even indulged in baths in wooden tubs filled by buckets of heated water. People either bathed naked or just wore their undergarments. They used tallow soaps blended with roses, lavender or almonds. They cleaned their teeth with toothpicks and then rinsed with cold water or wine. People chewed parsley to freshen their breath.

ADVERTISEMENT

Men wore separate trouser legs, each fastened to his belt or underwear. A woman's dress also had separate sleeves to attach.

ROBIN HOOD HAT

PAGEBOY HAIRCUT

Stoat

ERMINE

HOOD

Ermine

The aristocracy lined their winter clothing with fur. Small animals such as squirrels, martens, sables and stoats were highly valued for their fur. An ermine cloak, usually a symbol of royalty, was made from the winter coat of the stoat and was trimmed with its black and white tail.

10 Tudors

SLIM WAISTS & ROUNDED BELLIES

Tudor tailors waved goodbye to the simpler fashions of medieval times. The favourite material was now soft velvet, which in its embroidered form is known as velvet brocade. Low necklines had translucent linen inserts stitched into the bodices for modesty. Strings of pearls were sewn onto the dresses of rich women. The pointed shoes of the Middle Ages were now a thing of the past – shoes now had rounded toes. Queen Elizabeth I of England was fond of lace ruffs and sumptuous robes made of heavy fabrics, embroidered with gold and silver threads.

But how good it looks, Your Majesty.

I must sit ...my dress is so heavy!

Wow! Look – silk stockings.

Elizabeth I

Henry VIII

Oh...my knees!

BROOCHES

LADY OF THE COURT

RUFF

More passion, Romeo!

ACTORS IN EVERYDAY DRESS

ACTORS IN COSTUME

PADDED BREECHES

FOR BEAUTIFUL SKIN: *Our cosmetics are made with crushed pearls!*

William Shakespeare

Essential fashion

Decorative cut sleeves with the underdress peeping through; ❶ a gold hairnet, ❷ lace handkerchief ❸ and a lace-up jerkin. ❹

Stockings

King Henry VIII really was given a pair of embroidered silk stockings by the Spanish ambassador. He prized them more highly than a gift of a coach and horses!

Leonardo da Vinci

Mmm... it all comes down to cones, triangles and circles . . .

Meanwhile, in Italy, whilst painting Renaissance ladies, Leonardo da Vinci came to realise that the proportions of the human body fitted into quite specific shapes. Clothing design would soon be governed by strict rules of geometry.

Pay attention to shape!

The ideal beauty of this time was a slim-waisted woman with wide, childbearing hips. Corsets and bodices clinched in a woman's waist and flattened her chest. A hooped petticoat worn under the skirt completed her perfect shape.

A round belly was a 'must' for the elegantly dressed man. Those who were unfashionably slim had to add padding to their belly and their bottoms, too. This fashionably wider body girth meant that chairs had to be made bigger to accommodate the sitter.

Fashion fads

- Young men liked to show off their muscular calves but older men chose longer garments for respectability.
- Ladies took to shaving back their hairline to create a fashionably high forehead.
- The starched, concertina folds of a lace ruff were kept in shape by a wire frame. Ruffs had the effect of making the head look as though it was sat on a platter.

Cor...this stinks!

Festive clothes

How often were such clothes washed? Never! Only underwear ever got rinsed!

II 17th Century

ROUNDED SILHOUETTES

17th century fashion was based on its admiration of grandiose beauty and rounded silhouettes. The ideal of beauty consisted of a plump, cherubic figure with lavish clothes and hairstyles. Women even slept sitting up in order not to ruin their hair! Boys and girls were both dressed in the same clothes as grown women.

Why can't I dress like Dad?

It could be worse, little brother – at least it's not pink!

Noblemen and women wore heeled shoes, decorated with buckles, bows and pompoms. Buckles and ostrich feathers also featured strongly on hats. Gloves were worn to accessorise the costumes of both men and women.

Darling, my new dress is beautiful ...but we'll have to get the chairs enlarged again!

HANDMADE LACE COLLAR

Have you seen my powder compact?

No, but I could lend you my lipstick?

Men and women wore powdered wigs and make-up. 17th century aristocracy liked nothing better than hosting costly balls where everyone could show off.

HELPFUL HINTS:
HOW TO ACHIEVE THAT ATTENTION-GRABBING LOOK!

How to achieve that glamorous, attention-grabbing look.

1. Apply white powder to your skin. Be warned – it's made from lead so it's poisonous! If your skin ever starts to go yellow, just apply a heavier dusting of powder.

2. Darken your eyebrows or glue on strips of mouse skin instead. Use good quality glue so that they don't fall off!

3. Your hair should be worn in decorative ringlets… or wear a wig. Horse hair wigs are too coarse, so find a woman who is poor enough to sell you her hair to make into a wig.

PERFUME BOTTLE

BRIGHT-RED LIPSTICK

POWDER COMPACT

POWDER PUFF FOR APPLYING POWDER

Women's wide skirts were very problematic! It was difficult to see where they ended so many a vase or ornament was sent flying. Dancing was a tricky business, too –men often complained that they couldn't get close to a woman because of her huge skirts.

RIBBON LACING

LACE CRAVAT

THREE-CORNERED HAT

CORSET

EMBROIDERED DRESS FRONT

HOOPED UNDERSKIRT

STOCKINGS

How to dress properly for a ball

Late 17th century clothing was defined by lace, ribbons, frills, fake flowers and pearls. A top layer was added like a coat. The bosom was concealed by an embroidered dress front, pinned to the corset. Waists were nipped in with a corset or bustier, reinforced with whale bone. With dresses as large as a table, ladies often had to pass through doorways sideways. This enormous shape was created by a hooped construction worn underneath the dress, with a series of petticoats. A gentleman's coat was finished off with an opulent lace cravat at his neck.

THE 'HEIGHT' OF FASHION

Walk tall in our fashionable footwear. These heeled shoes will stop the hem of your dress getting wet.

The Little Slipper Shoe Shop, 15 Golden Lane

Shoes were made of velvet, brocade, satin or soft leather. They were adorned with ribbons, precious stones and pearls.

WIDE SELECTION OF DRESS SHOES: *Get ready for the ball!*

SUSPENDER

MEN'S DRAWERS

PETTICOAT

LADIES' DRAWERS

If a lady tripped or fell over, her wide skirts were likely to reveal all that was underneath. So ladies wore pretty drawers and a petticoat under their dresses. Gentlemen also wore drawers decorated with lace, and stockings that were held up with coloured ribbons.

The **SECRET LANGUAGE** *of the fan!*

I want to talk to you.

Kiss me.

Someone is watching us.

Go away!

Don't forget me!

I love...someone else.

Court clothes

1700 – 1800 AD

FLOWERS, GOLD & ORNAMENT

The elaborate clothes of the French court now set the fashion scene. Small floral patterns were popular, and white and gold were the favoured colours. While less sophisticated people continued to wear the old fashions, the extravagant aristocracy borrowed from the French to create their own new style. Wearing tighter bodices and big panniered dresses, ladies looked like fragile porcelain dolls. Gentlemen wore jackets in light pastel shades with decorative buttons. Jackets had wires inside the fabric to make them sit well at the back, and had exaggerated cuffs. The jacket, shirt, waistcoat, tie and trousers of this period form the basis of a gentleman's suit today.

CATALOGUE
*SPRING
& SUMMER*

Up into the waves!

Bird's paradise

Immersed in feathers

Lace fontange

Comfort first

Fruit dream

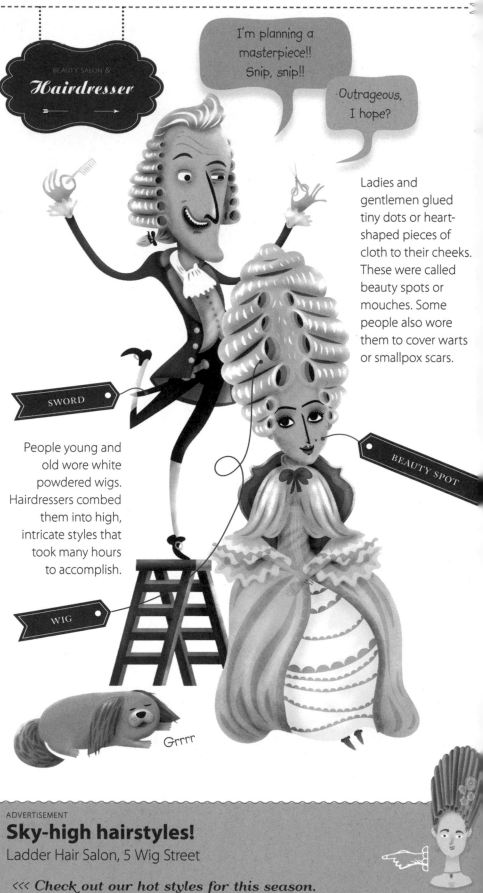

BEAUTY SALON &
Hairdresser

I'm planning a masterpiece!! Snip, snip!!

Outrageous, I hope?

SWORD

WIG

Grrrr

Ladies and gentlemen glued tiny dots or heart-shaped pieces of cloth to their cheeks. These were called beauty spots or mouches. Some people also wore them to cover warts or smallpox scars.

BEAUTY SPOT

People young and old wore white powdered wigs. Hairdressers combed them into high, intricate styles that took many hours to accomplish.

Aristocrats

At home in their mansions, ladies would wear comfortable but elegant house-coats. Wigs were a haven for lice so ladies would carry a decorative scratcher in the shape of a little golden hand. At home, they wore embroidered caps to conceal what little remained of their own hair.

SCRATCHER

Bothered by troublesome insects?

Wolfi

Wolfgang Amadeus Mozart (1756-1791)

Famous figures of the period

Important personalities of this period include the composer, Wolfgang Amadeus Mozart and Madame de Pompadour, who gave her name to a little round handbag.

POMPADOUR BAG

Getting personal...

Doctors thought water was harmful and full of germs so everyone gave it a wide berth. Body odour was concealed by the strong scent of orange blossom, or apple with cinnamon and cloves. The first men's cologne was produced at this time, as was pomade, a scented hair dressing. Make-up remover did not exist – it was just left on the face.

Madame de Pompadour

13 Empire inspired *1780 - 1820 AD*

PUFFED SLEEVES

Hurrah, I can breathe!

FOLDING FAN

HIGH WAISTLINE

LONG GLOVES

LADIES' TRAVEL CLOAK

A FASHION REVOLUTION IN SOFT COLOURS

Between 1780 and 1820, European fashions altered dramatically. Exciting new ideas of freedom and social reform were in the air. Ladies' fashions of this period became softer, lighter and more natural-looking. Casting off their corsets, ladies could now move and breathe without restriction. The popularity of travelling by horse and carriage led to the creation of the first travel bags and handbags. Pale skin was still fashionable, so ladies wore bonnets to keep the sun off their faces. Different coloured ribbons were added to a hat to accessorise it with various outfits or shoes. Ladies wore their hair in a centre parting with curled ringlets at each side.

Unlike their powdered forefathers, elegant young men washed daily and paid great attention to all aspects of their clothing. They wore tall, shiny top hats, carried smart walking sticks and polished their shoes with expensive champagne.

Young ladies favoured dresses made of very light, sheer fabrics, accompanied by colourful muslin or cashmere shawls. White was popular, but shades of beige, lilac and lavender also crept in, as well as patterned fabrics. Children's clothes became less restrictive, too : girls wore shorter skirts with pantaloons and boys finally got to wear trousers.

TOP HAT

WALKING STICK

TROUSERS WITH A "FALL FRONT"

A well-sewn tailcoat with two rows of brass buttons.

The revolution in fashion also led to the popularity of fashion magazines. Every woman wanted to keep up with the latest trends.

MEN'S TRAVEL OVERCOAT

The French ruler Napoleon Bonaparte brought back many new fashions from his travels. On his triumphant return to Paris as Emperor, he made the city into a fashion capital. His wife, Josephine, became the fashion icon of the time.

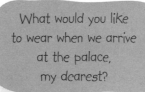

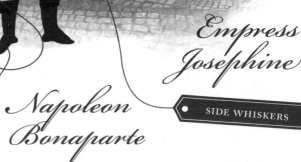

Empress Josephine

Napoleon Bonaparte

SIDE WHISKERS

EPAULETTES

14 Romanticism

1820 – 1860 AD

HAUTE COUTURE & WASP WAISTS

True romantics wandered, composed poems and pondered the deeper questions of life, death and love. Romantic period novels sold like hot cakes so it's not surprising that people's eyesight suffered. Spectacles, a sign of a true intellectual, were held up to the eyes on a kind of stalk. People also wore pince-nez or a round lens that hung around their neck on a chain.

PINCE-NEZ

Men wore striped or checked trousers that overhung their shoes. Women aspired to having an hourglass figure, and stuffed the sleeves of their dresses with fine duck or goose down.

FOR YOUR LOVED ONE: A LOCKET WITH YOUR PORTRAIT AND A LOCK OF HAIR SECRETED INSIDE.

SLEEVES STUFFED WITH FEATHERS

My dolly rides sidesaddle.

This is a 'boys only' horse!

GAITERS

DON'T MISS THIS 'TIMELY' **INNOVATION**

You'll never be late with a pocket watch on a chain!

Schoolgirls were taught to sew, knit, crochet and embroider. They could also use one of the first sewing machines to make their own beautiful trousseau.

BOAT NECKLINE

HOOPSKIRT

WORTH

TIGHTLY LACED BODICE

BOW TIE

PROTECTIVE HEM

TAILCOAT

Empress Sissi

Charles Worth

Haute couture

Charles Worth is considered to be the first fashion designer and the founder of high fashion (known as 'haute couture'). He made evening dresses for the beautiful Austro-Hungarian empress, Sissi. He also invented the bustle, a petticoat that emphasised a lady's posterior. Its steel structure was later replaced with padding.

Empress Sissi wore tight-laced leather corsets made in Paris and her slender wasp waist became the height of fashion. Ladies were laced into ever tighter corsets, causing them to suffer stomach ulcers and fainting fits. Men, too, wanted slim waists and wore corsets under their coats.

INDUSTRIAL REVOLUTION!

THE FIRST FACTORIES WERE FILLED WITH **WEAVING AND KNITTING MACHINES**, MAKING TEXTILE MANUFACTURING MUCH EASIER!

ADVERTISEMENT

A TOTAL HIT

Wear ankle boots and make foot and leg strain a thing of the past!

RIDING HAT

RIDING HABIT

DIVIDED SKIRT

Sissi had her own gymnasium at the palace, and was better on horseback than many men. She rode sidesaddle, wearing a dress. Later, ladies daringly wore a divided skirt or even men's trousers to ride more comfortably in a man's saddle.

Edwardian Era

1901 – 1910 AD

THE 'TRAVEL BUG' & INNOVATIVE MACHINES

Slowly but surely machines took over some people's hard work. They used their free time to travel and take walks in the fresh air. Visiting distant relatives was now far easier. Wealthy ladies travelled with a large wardrobe of clothes as it was customary to change outfits frequently throughout the day.

Do try not to get dirty, darling! We still haven't got a washing machine at home!

SMART DRESS

Hmmph...is that a hint?

PLATFORM

&

Wear that new dress to welcome your husband back from his travels!

GLOVES

Such speed!

FASHION EXPRESS

TOP HAT

SIDE WHISKERS

Hat exhibition

Women's and girls' hats came in all shapes and colours, and were lavishly decorated with ribbons, silk flowers and exotic bird feathers. The feathers of the snowy egret were as highly valued as gold. If conservationists had not stopped the hunting of egrets for their plumes, these birds would now be extinct.

Dress codes

The length of a skirt was not determined by the occasion or activity intended – all skirts were long! Skirts were often worn with a spencer, a short coat with gigot sleeves, often called 'leg o' mutton sleeves' because of their padded shape.

Gentlemen changed outfits frequently throughout the day, too. In daytime they dressed in lighter shades, while darker colours or black were favoured for evening wear. Men's trousers looked almost the same as they do today, although they were fastened by concealed buttons as zips had yet to be invented. A gentleman's footwear had significantly higher heels than today.

Concealed buttons in all our trousers!

Fashion Demands

One outfit for the morning tea party, another for the afternoon walk, a third for evening wear. And the weather had to be taken into consideration, too – umbrella or parasol? Finally, children were allowed to be children. They could now wear practical outdoor clothing instead of velvet jackets and white lace.

COLOURFUL TIE

STRAW HAT

DOUBLE-BREASTED JACKET

SAILOR DRESS

PARASOL

Sailor suits were originally intended for wear on boat rides or coastal walks. They gradually became the chosen style for bathing suits, too.

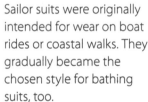

Oh! Look at the time and I'm still in my morning dress! What a disgrace! Quick children, I must dash home and change!

Good behaviour

Fashion was about more than just appearances. Natty dressers cared only about being admired but a gentleman, although perhaps not so well dressed, never forgets his manners. He always lifts his hat in greeting and wishes others 'good day'.

Stylish velocipedists

PENNY FARTHING

BICYCLE

THE SEASON HAS **STARTED!**

A lady's cycling costume comprised of a close-fitting jacket, a divided skirt, a straw hat with a veil and lace-up boots.

Gentlemen wore tweed jackets in brown pinstripe or check.

FLORIOGRAPHY FOR A GENTLEMAN
The language of flowers

Are you saying that I'm prickly and unpleasant?

Oh, no – my floriography has backfired!

FLORIOGRAPHY

Daisy = I like you.

Red rose = I love you.

Cactus = I will love you always.

Art Nouveau

1890 – 1910 AD

ART NOUVEAU STYLE INSPIRED BY NATURE

The natural undulating lines of a climbing plant or a woman's flowing hair often inspired Art Nouveau designs. Gowns made of translucent materials which were strewn with beads in unusual shades of yellows, blues and greens were extremely popular.

Book now!
WORLD PREMIERE!

THEATRE

FEATHER BOA

FOX FUR

Théâtre de Paris

Russian ballet
SCHEHERAZADE TODAY

A GUIDE FOR THEATRE-GOING GENTLEMEN!

Set the mood with a tailcoat, ❶ a high-collared shirt and white gloves. ❷ Have creases pressed into your trousers. ❸ Slick your hair down with brilliantine (a pomade made of petroleum jelly, beeswax or lard). ❹ It will give your hair an impressive shine. Don't forget your moustache – use special wax to twirl it carefully into shape. ❺ Add a top hat for the final touch! ❻

BOWLER HAT

TOP HAT

As fashionable society entered this French theatre to see the new ballet Scheherazade, little did they know that fashion, as they knew it, was about to be swept away!

Winds of the Orient

Russian ballerinas wearing airy, oriental costumes floated across the stage, as though borne aloft by the wings of a butterfly. Ladies looked on in breathless amazement. No doubt they, too, wished they could cast off their tight-fitting dresses to fly as free as a bird like the ballerinas.

Corsets pulled in the hips as well as the waist. This twisted a woman's body into an unnatural 'S' bend shape. This made her look a little like a duck: her chest swelled out at the front and her posterior did likewise at the back.

A SECRET ADMIRER OF THE 'NEW LOOK'?

Get yourself a comfortable dressing gown and hat in the oriental style.

Can-can

The exuberant Parisian can-can dancers brought more than a revolutionary dance to the cabaret. They were equally famous for their provocative corsets with garters and lace knickers.

THE SECRET OF AN ETHEREAL APPEARANCE:
a hidden corset

Such a bold fashion... but so exciting!

TASSELLED HANDBAG

GLASS BEADS

'S' BEND FIGURE

An icon of design

The French designer Paul Poiret was famous for his bold and imaginative creations. He enlivened the wardrobes of Europe with memorable items such as his feathered turban. He is considered a pioneer of Art Nouveau fashion.

VOGUE   No / 01

EXCLUSIVE INTERVIEW!

Paul Poiret

A BREATH OF FRESH AIR FOR FASHION

VOGUE: Mr Poiret, you're now renowned throughout the world as an innovative designer, but how did you start out in the industry?

PAUL POIRET: I come from humble origins. I was born to a cloth merchant in a poor part of Paris. However, I began sketching dress designs from a young age and quickly gained a name for myself in the trade.

V: You have freed women from tight corsets and given them clothing the like of which has never been seen before. Can you take us through your work?

PP: My idea was to move away from the stuffy, stiff designs of the past. When I set up my own fashion house, I began to create loose-fitting and flamboyant clothes for slim figures, such as my famous kimonos.

V: Fabulous! Thank you for the interview, and take care of your muse!

INTERVIEW   11

A legendary magazine

Vogue magazine was devoted entirely to fashion trends and fashion news. Ladies' hearts jumped for joy when it was first published in New York. Fashion lovers still read Vogue today, more than a hundred years after its first issue.

PAUL POIRET'S CREATIONS:

TRANSLUCENT STRIPED DRESS

FUR TRIMMED COAT

Underwear

Not all women wanted to spend their day squeezed into a horribly tight corset. Fortunately this new fashion was kinder, allowing women to wear much more comfortable and looser types of underwear. They could wear long shifts ❶ or pantaloons ❷ which were ideal for cyclists. Ladies who couldn't quite abandon the habit of being clamped in place by a corset could even replace it with a brassiere and an elasticated girdle! ❸

How wonderfully comfortable!

TIP:
Express your admiration with an enchanting gift of Art Nouveau jewellery!

Glittering dragonfly wings, iridescent peacock feathers and bright-coloured petals inspired not only fashion designers, but also jewellers. Motifs based on nature soon featured in necklaces, brooches and combs.

PARTY DRESS WITH ROSES

DRESS WITH WIRED LAMPSHADE TUNIC

ORIENTAL DRESS WITH TURKISH TROUSERS

ORIENTAL-STYLE EVENING DRESS

The Roaring 20s

1920 – 1929 AD

FEATHERED HEADBAND

BEADED DRESS

FRINGE DRESS

HAVE A BALL IN A **COCKTAIL DRESS**!

DANCE FASHION WITH A JAZZ RHYTHM

The hardships and sorrows of the First World War left no time for fashion. But, as the 1920s dawned, people could again make merry and dance until dawn! Heels clacked to the rhythms of jazz and the girls' knee-length dresses were ablaze with beads and tassels. These straight shoulder-strapped garments later became known as 'cocktail dresses'. The new fashion was bold, playful and free-spirited. Women also began to wear make-up again.

Hemlines rose, and hair was cut into a fashionably short 'bob'. The new style caused quite a stir with mothers and grandmothers who were still draped from head to toe in the old-fashioned style.

TOQUE

Every day newspapers carried photographs of mobsters on the run or beautiful actresses wearing their hair fashionably bobbed or with a 'marcel wave'. Small hats, called toques, were popular.

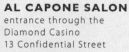
Charlie Chaplin

Many tried to imitate the most famous comic actor of the silent movies. There was even a 'Best Charlie Chaplin' competition. Chaplin, who entered this contest in secret, finished third!

HELPFUL HINTS:
THE SILENT MOVIE STAR LOOK!

Pluck out your eyebrows and draw them on with a thin pencil line. Make your skin look paler and your eyes more bewitching by accentuating them with smoky shadows and black outines. Use mascara – a new beauty product from selected cosmetic salons. Apply ruby-red lipstick by hand or using a stencil.

'LITTLE BLACK DRESS'

Coco Chanel

Coco Chanel, perhaps the best-known fashion designer of all time, became famous for her 'little black dress', worn with pearl accessories. This simple garment still forms the foundation of many women's wardrobes today.

Jeanne Lanvin

The initial success of designer Jeanne Lanvin arose from garments she made for her daughter. Wealthy clients who wanted copies for their own child, were soon ordering clothes for themselves, too. She chose colours specifically to suit the personal attributes of the woman she was dressing. She didn't aspire to the fashionable 'boyish' look; her designs were softer.

18 The Forties

All morning, afternoon and evening wear is banned! Long skirts are a scandalous waste of material, and so are pockets!

Elsa Schiaparelli

IMPROVISE & ECONOMISE

In the early 1940s, when the Second World War broke out, the message was "Save, save, save"! Clothes and shoes were in short supply and people queued for hours to get them. All clothes looked almost the same: dull shades of grey or brown in angular styles, akin to military uniforms.

SHEATH DRESS

SILK GOWN

Glamour

Occasionally a designer came up with an unusual design, like Schiaparelli's hat in the shape of a shoe. It went well with a sheath dress, which certainly didn't waste any fabric. Silk was needed for parachutes so only famous actresses wore glamorous silk gowns. Necessity being the mother of invention, women altered old clothes to create new 'models' and thought up endless substitutes for expensive or scarce goods.

A TIP FOR YOU

Keep a shine on your shoes!

BLACK
SHOE POLISH

USE SHOE POLISH!

After the War

When the war finally ended, cars and aeroplanes were no longer just for military purposes. Men and women were fascinated by flight. Some learned to drive a vehicle and then even dared to fly planes. Inside the cockpit they just swapped their motoring cap and wide trousers for high lace-up leather boots and a leather flying helmet, and then it was up, up and away!

LEATHER HELMET

Cheerful Colours

Like people, fashion became more cheerful after the war. Men swapped their military uniforms for elegant sports jackets and smart hats. The latest in footwear for men was comfortable moccasins.

Children's fashion had flair, too. Girls wore simple dresses with collars, and boys wore short trousers with braces.

ZIP

Three cheers for zips!

There was even time for sport! A new invention – the zip – made dressing much easier. Can you imagine how long it took to undo the buttons on a ski suit to go to the toilet? Zips were a huge success!

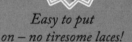
HOUNDSTOOTH PATTERN

CARPET BAG

ADVERTISEMENT

Is that handbag real Persian carpet or just an old rug?

FOX-FUR STOLE

Coats, hats and carpetbags, some of which were made out of old rugs, became the height of winter fashion.

2 in 1

The Fifties

1950 – 1959 AD

A FASHION FOR BILLOWING SKIRTS

Postwar optimism swept bright colours and patterns into fashion. Modern printing machines and new artificial fibres that absorbed dyes better created colours and patterns that really stood out. Girls twirled around in their full skirts, trying to look like the film star, Marilyn Monroe. The 'tough guy' look was all the rage: T-shirt, leather jacket, jeans and a greased back quiff, just like the king of rock 'n' roll – Elvis!

Elvis Presley

Only youuu...

He's the King...

Why's he so great...?

Christian Dior

A Fashion Revolution

Christian Dior, a revolutionary figure in fashion design, was born into a family of fertiliser merchants. But he decided to follow fashion, not fertilisers. His signature style of full skirts and waspy waists with thin belts led the way. Women loved it! Bold shapes underlay every style: suits that resembled the letter 'Y', full skirted dresses with an 'A'-line shape and straight dresses that looked like a letter 'H'.

'A' LINE

'H' LINE

'Y' LINE

Marilyn Monroe

Audrey Hepburn, the fragile, dark-haired actress with almond-shaped eyes, made this "little black dress" famous in the film 'Breakfast at Tiffany's'. It was designed by Givenchy fashion house. It became the second most expensive film costume ever to be auctioned in aid of charity. Marilyn Monroe's white dress from the film 'The Seven Year Itch' sold for even more.

GORGEOUS, EVEN IN A POTATO SACK

A journalist once said to Marilyn Monroe: "You'd even look good in a potato sack!" The actress didn't hesitate - photographs of the famous beauty wearing a potato sack soon circled the globe. The company whose name was on the sack sent Marilyn a supply of potatoes!

Audrey Hepburn

The Barbie doll dates back to the 1950s. Originally she was created to show girls what was new in fashion.

BARBIE DOLL

Daring Coco

The most famous women's suit was designed by Coco Chanel. Women could now be beautiful, elegant and comfortable at the same time. The designer's legendary perfume, Chanel no. 5, provided the final touch!

When Mum was out, many a curious young lady abandoned her girlish shoes and socks and secretly tried on Mum's high heels, lipstick and nail varnish…

SUIT BY COCO CHANEL

Previously Paris had reigned supreme, but London and Milan now became equally famous fashion capitals - all thanks to knitwear. Sweaters, pullovers and cardigans spread in popularity, as did polo-necks and knitted waistcoats. Knitting had arrived!

Milk bar

PULLOVER

DRESS WITH FULL SKIRT

ARE YOU LOOKING FOR PRACTICAL CLOTHING FOR WORK AND RELAXATION?

A cardigan covers most occasions!

ZIP-UP CARDIGAN

TROUSERS WITH PRESSED PLEATS

Women were workers as well as housewives. No matter their role, women always kept up their appearances. Red lipstick was highly popular. Shoulder-length hair was curled with rollers or curling tongs and held in place with hairgrips or scarves. At work, long hair was tied up with a ribbon or covered by a headscarf for safety reasons.

After hard work, some delicious cake!

Brilliant whites were the fashion in tennis. Comfortable tennis shoes became increasingly popular, too.

On hot summer days the swimming pool beckoned but even there, fashion ruled. The usual one-piece swimsuit was about to be superceded by a scandalous breakthrough in the world of swimwear - the new bikini! Only the bravest girls dared to wear it.

ONE-PIECE SWIMSUIT

Men's swimming trunks usually reached up to the waist and might also have a belt or a small pocket.

BIKINI

SPLASH!
Cool off and get a tan!

Nice bathing cap!

Are you ready yet?

SUNDRESS

Ladies wore headscarves to protect their hair from the sun, and elegant sunglasses to protect their eyes. Colourful bathing caps decorated with plastic flowers or tassels were worn to prevent carefully groomed hairstyles from getting wet. Polka dots were really popular as were stripes, and cherry or strawberry patterns.

The Sixties

1960 – 1969 AD

The Beatles

Anyone got a comb?

MOP TOP HAIR STYLE

FLOWER POWER & MOONWALKS

The Sixties were a time when ordinary people did extraordinary things. Suddenly fashion was being determined by teenagers. A mishmash of styles evolved with something for everyone. The Beatles emerged with long hair and a new sound for the era. Not only did they launch a new style in music, but John, Paul, George and Ringo also introduced a fashion trend – a black roll-neck sweater or white shirt worn with a smart suit with a collarless jacket. A rougher, more rebellious rock sound made icons of the Rolling Stones, who wore leather waistcoats and tight trousers.

BE BEWITCHING
...with fabulous false eyelashes!

Beauty comes in many forms. Don't try to be someone you're not!

The Rolling Stones

Twiggy

The model Twiggy became a fashion idol. She had a slim, boyish figure, wore short mini skirts and framed her eyes with three sets of false eyelashes. Twiggy was naturally slender but some girls, desperate to copy her, stopped eating and many ended up in hospital. Twiggy later campaigned about the eating disorder, anorexia.

Twiggy

The sixties was a decade of dramatic change in fashion. The perfectly groomed style of Jackie Kennedy, America's First Lady until 1963, had given way to the hippy flower power look by 1967.

Long-haired hippies professed love, peace and freedom. They wore tie-dyed T-shirts, wooden beads and embroidered, bell-bottom jeans. Sometimes it was hard to tell boys from girls. They adored nature: flowers, animals and people.

Jacqueline Kennedy

I see hats...like planets in outer space!

Pierre Cardin

Everyone watched in suspense as man first set foot on the Moon. Space travel became a new source of inspiration. Fashion designers, including Pierre Cardin began to create clothes out of perspex, strips of metal and plastic wrapping.

SAY NO TO FURS

Beautiful actress Brigitte Bardot would never have been seen in a real fur coat.

She held the view that in a materialist age it was stupid to kill animals for their fur and skin. She is still a firm campaigner for animal rights today.

BE INSPIRED BY BB

Bouffant hair, large plastic earrings and thick false eyelashes were all in fashion. Girls liked to wear miniskirts with long, colourful knee socks. Attention-grabbing colours were 'in'!

BRIGHT **COLOUR** ALL ROUND!

FALSE EYELASHES

Oh no, I've lost a set of eyelashes!

Here - I'll lend you mine...

COLOURFUL KNEE SOCKS

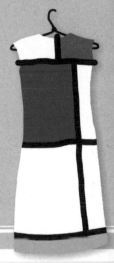
Brigitte Bardot

BB DRESSED BY THE WORLD'S BEST DESIGNERS

❶ This dress made of small metal discs was designed by Paco Rabanne. ❷ Transparent dress by fashion designer, YvesSaint-Laurent. ❸ A paper dress inferring that fashion is beautiful but short-lived. ❹ Pop art by Yves Saint-Laurent for that geometric look. ❺ Pop art for comic book fans.

DISCO FEVER!

If Sixties' fashion seemed eccentric to you, then take a look at what people wore ten years later! Shiny, elasticated, artificial materials 'ruled'. There was an abundance of glitter, sequins and eye-catching vibrant colours. Spacesuit themes still lingered on from the last decade. The Seventies, in fact, became known as the 'tasteless decade' and the styles of the time were called 'anti-fashion'.

Show me what you wear and I can tell what music you listen to. People wore practically anything, but their taste in music was often reflected in the type of clothes they chose to wear.

FUNKY

BREAK DANCE

POP

High platform shoes were fashionable but hardly practical except for walking through puddles – your feet stayed dry! The blue jeans mania swept across the world. Denim, originally a tough, hardwearing fabric worn by cowboys, now became the chosen material for jackets, dresses, skirts, trousers…

DISCO

PLATFORM SHOES

VIVIENNE WESTWOOD

PUNK, PUNK, PUNK!

Going against the flow

Not everyone loved the garish, disco fashion trends. Many sought an alternative identity by their choice of music or clothes. Designer Vivienne Westwood found inspiration in things that others rejected. She and other 'punk' fans created high fashion out of items such as ripped T-shirts, tartan, fishnet stockings and leather jackets studded with pins.

DISCO RULES

GOTH

INDIE

ROCK

PUNK

COUNTRY

This is the 'gents', luv!

PERMED HAIR

FLARED SLEEVES

JUMPSUIT

Men's chests were bared in shirts, fashionably half-buttoned. Bell-bottomed trousers were the latest look along with flared sleeves on shirts and blouses. One-piece jumpsuits were a fashion hit. Often, it was hard to tell men and women apart. The singer David Bowie went a step further by wearing make-up as well as his flamboyant costumes.

DAVID BOWIE

The Eighties

1980 – 1989 AD

PLASTIC MANIA

Court shoes with stiletto heels, and wide, exaggerated shoulders became the dominant look for Eighties' women. No jacket, blouse, coat or dress came without shoulder pads! Men wore ties and colourful braces, and crocodile-skin moccasins. Fortunately for crocodiles, the leather was mostly imitation!

A HOLEY T-SHIRT?
How embarrassing…
No… it's high fashion!

Bell-bottoms gave way to skinny drainpipes. The ideal jeans now looked as though they had spent a month going mouldy in a dank cellar.

SHOULDER PADS

HOLEY T-SHIRT

CROCODILE-SKIN HANDBAG

CROCODILE-SKIN MOCCASINS

MARBLE-WASH JEANS

DENIM JACKET

Sport is cool!

Roller skating and aerobics were hugely popular. A tracksuit ❶ with matching headband ❷ was a 'must' along with a rucksack or bum bag. ❸ Trainers or sneakers, ideally with fluorescent laces, completed the look! ❹

For exercising, girls wore bright-coloured leggings, ruffle skirts, or legwarmers. ❺ Patterned, multicoloured leggings looked great with wide belts or crop tops. ❻

Girls wore romantic-style dresses, and lipsticks that ranged from pale pink shades to burgundy red. Boys wore sweaters draped casually over their shoulders.

'Big Hair'

'Big hair' was the look to kill for! Men and women who lacked a good head of hair had their locks permed and curled. Men also wore their hair short on top and long at the neck. The most fashionable hair colour was blond.

Michael Jackson

The singer and dancer Michael Jackson, known as the 'king of pop', was a genius of rhythm, dance and fashion. Today, black loafers worn with white socks would definitely be 'out', but in the eighties Jackson's style was copied by thousands of his fans.

BE TRENDY!

Replace gold and silver with these 'must have' plastic accessories:

- heart-shaped glasses
- star earrings
- Smiley badges
- plastic bangles and rings
- friendship bracelets
- charm bracelets
- holey T-shirts

CURLERS

FINGERLESS GLOVES

'BIG HAIR'

BALLOON SKIRT

TULLE SKIRT

RUBBER SANDALS

PLASTIC HANDBAG

The Nineties

1990 – 1999 AD

LONDON STYLE!

In the Nineties people generally wore loose, comfortable clothing for work and leisure. Denim jeans, dresses and hats were hugely popular. Originally invented in 1979, the Walkman had now become a must-have accessory. The great-grandfather of today's MP3 players was a big hit, being the first small, portable device for playing music.

HIT OF THE SEASON: *Denim!*

DOGGY OVERCOAT

WALKMAN

BASEBALL CAP

DUNGAREES

DENIM DRESS

London youth came up with a style known as 'grunge'. The principle was simply to look as though you just didn't care. Most looked as though they had just crawled out of a dustbin – much to the despair of most parents!

FLANNEL SHIRT

TORN JEANS

HOW TO BE GRUNGE!

Get yourself:

- a faded second-hand T-shirt
- a flannel shirt to tie around your waist
- frayed jeans, torn shorts and a checked skirt
- long, bedraggled hair
- a baseball cap worn back to front
- round glasses with coloured frames
- Converse canvas sneakers or heavy-duty Dr Martens shoes

1

2

Marc Jacobs

Young designers had an interest in this fashion, too. Marc Jacobs designed a number of expensive items in this style . . . and his fashion house Perry Ellis promptly sacked him. Only a fool would pay money for such rags! But the designer was ahead of his time as grunge style caught on – even with celebrities.

DR MARTENS SHOES

CONVERSE SNEAKERS

Madonna mia!

The flamboyant pop singer Madonna, became a symbol of the time. Her iconic corset with its exaggerated, conical bosoms was designed by Jean-Paul Gaultier.

Jean Paul Gaultier

Madonna

Meet the queen of pop – I designed her...

DENIM HAT

Those who didn't want to follow the 'grunge' fashion style could let their imagination run wild. How about high pigtails **1** a pineapple-style on the top of the head **2** topknots and fashionable John Lennon specs **3** or butterfly clips and glitter eye make-up? **4** Or a head full of braids and beads, bright-blue eyelashes and a choker **5** around the neck! Boys experimented with shavers, perms, gels and bleaches. **6**

SCHOOL

Back to your desks, girls!

FRIZZY HAIR

To get a fashionable frizzy hairstyle, just unbraid your plaits!

Contemporary Fashion

AD 2000 – present day

UNIQUE CHOICES

Today's fashion can change from one day to the next. Yesterday people were wearing tight blouses…today it could be baggy tops. But no one has to follow fashion. There are no hard and fast rules to govern what must be worn. Everyone can choose what suits them or simply what they like best. Contemporary fashion is free: wear clothes that make you feel most comfortable, regardless of the activity or occasion.

Some styles are strikingly familiar, aren't they? Almost everything that is worn today has been worn at some time in the past.

The **modern man's suit** ❶ has remained essentially the same since Victorian times and the jazz age of the Twenties.

Contemporary Japanese fashion has come a long way from the traditional kimono of the samurai and the geisha. But were the **platform shoes** ❷ of the Seventies inspired by footwear from ancient China?

Women have worn **corsets** ❸ from the Renaissance to the 1950s. In the past, corsets were an item of underwear, however they are often a feature of modern party dresses now.

Remember when **jeans** and **peaked caps** first saw the light of day? In the Fifties. ❹

Unisex fashion ❺ is for girls and boys.

❻ Classics never go out of fashion. **Handbags** have existed since the 18th century, as have **high-waisted dresses** ❼.

Retro fashion (also known as vintage) ❽ is so popular that it keeps coming back.

The first **high-heeled shoes**? The Renaissance got there first! ❾

COLOURED NAILS? THE CELTS GOT THERE FIRST!!

Eco fashion

Clothing, often made of natural materials like cotton, wool or linen. Eco fashion also includes jeans and bags produced from recycled bottles or chocolate-bar wrappers.

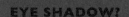

ECO T-SHIRT

Zip

Today it is hard to imagine clothes without easy-fastening zips yet the zip was only invented in the Forties!

EYE SHADOW?
*Hardly new is it?
The Ancient
Egyptians used it!*

WHERE DID THAT PARTY DRESS GO?

Spray-on clothing could meet all your fashion needs! Just clean it off whenever you want to create another great design..

FASHION TO ORDER

Alexander McQueen's butterfly hat – a design that won't fly off in all directions!!

It's so old it's new!

Hipsters, who are people that follow the latest trends in culture, ⑩ like to revive fashions of the past. They love all that is retro, including old bicycles.

Harem pants ⑪ inspired by the Orient look great with **flip-flops** ⑫ - footwear that may have originated from ancient Japan.

Don't forget what the English poet Percy Bysshe Shelley used to say:

"You're never fully dressed without a smile."

FASHION OF THE FUTURE

Who knows, maybe one day we'll wear intelligent clothing that will fasten or unfasten depending on whether we are hot or cold, like the futuristic designs of Hussein Chalayan. These clothes could be powered by the energy we generate while walking.

HIPSTER

Around the Fashion World

Let's remind ourselves... of how fashion has changed over time and across continents, from the beginning to the present day.

It's hot...

Ave Caesar!

PREHISTORY

ANCIENT EGYPT

ANCIENT ROME

ANCIENT GREECE

CELTS

CHINA

JAPAN

INDIA

TUDOR

MIDDLE AGES

17TH CENTURY

COURT CLOTHES

69

EMPIRE INSPIRED STYLES

ROMANTICISM

ART NOUVEAU

EDWARDIAN ERA

ROARING 20S

FORTIES

FIFTIES

SIXTIES

EIGHTIES

SEVENTIES

NINETIES

PRESENT DAY

71

Be inspired... by women who set the tone for contemporary fashion.

Jennifer Lopez
She has a liking for bright colours and seductively figure-hugging designs that accentuate her femininity.

Victoria Beckham
Her designer collections radiate confidence and simplicity.

Rihanna
Her fashion taste is bold and playful. Like a chameleon: you never know what to expect from her next!

Kate Moss
Black is chic! Apart from black, she has a liking for animal patterns and loves men's hats.

Mary-Kate & Ashley Olsen
Fans of non-traditional, bohemian styles with playful, fun accessories for added oomph!.

Lady Gaga
Likes to provoke and cross fashion boundaries. Sees herself as a walking work of art.

Anne Hathaway
Promotes a subtle, boyish style of dress.

Kate, Duchess of Cambridge
Her favourite 'official' look includes classic jackets accessorised with fetching hats.

Michelle Obama
America's first lady believes in elegance and comfort. She's not afraid of vivid colours.

Swimwear

300 BC · 1830 · 1870

1930 · 1920 · 1900 · 1890

1935 · 1945 · 1955 · PRESENT DAY

Ladies' Hats

●--- MIDDLE AGES ---- TUDOR -------- 17TH CENTURY -------- EMPIRE INSPIRED ------- EDWARDIAN ERA ------ 1920

●--- PRESENT DAY ------- 1990 --------- 1970 ------- 1950 --------- 1940 -------- 1930

Hairstyles

●--- ANCIENT EGYPT ----- MIDDLE AGES ------- TUDOR ------ 18TH CENTURY ------- EMPIRE INSPIRED ------ ART NOUVEAU

●--- 1990 ------- 1980 -------- 1970 ------ 1960 -------- 1940 ------- 1920

Wedding Dresses

EMPIRE INSPIRED — ROMANTICISM — LATE VICTORIAN ERA — ART NOUVEAU

1960 — 1950 — 1930 — 1920

1970 — 1980 — 1990 — PRESENT DAY

Jean Paul Gaultier

Calvin Klein

Christian Dior

Hussein Chalayan

Alexander McQueen

Issey Miyake

Valentino

Ralph Lauren

Vera Wang

Versace

John Galliano

Yves Saint-Laurent

Givenchy

Coco Chanel

Karl Lagerfeld

Marc Jacobs

Vivienne Westwood

Mary Quant

Pierre Cardin

Giorgio Armani

Stella McCartney

Shoes you need to know

Vivienne Westwood

Charlotte Olympia

Christian Louboutin

Giuseppe Zanotti

Melissa by V. Westwood

Joanne Stoker

Alexander McQueen

Jimmy Choo

Antonio Berardi

Manolo Blahnik

Handbags you need to know

Louis Vuitton Speedy 30

Alexander McQueen
Skull Clutch

Longchamp Tote Bag

Fendi Baguette

Bottega
Veneta Campana

Chloé Paraty

Hermès Birkin

Lady Dior

Mulberry Alexa

Chanel 2.55

Glossary

Celts
Groups of people in Iron Age and Medieval Europe who spread their languages and cultures into Ireland and Scotland, among other places.

China
A vast country in Asia that is home to over 1 billion people. It is one of the oldest civilisations in the world, having been ruled for most of its history by a succession of hereditary monarchies known as dynasties.

Edwardian era
The period of the reign of King Edward VII in Great Britain, from 1901 to 1910. It was a time marked by conspicuous wealth, the importing of extravagant fashion trends from Europe, and increasing unrest among the working-classes and women.

Egypt
A country located between the northeast corner of Africa and the southwest corner of Asia, mostly within the Nile Valley. It was home to the civilisation of Ancient Egypt where pharaohs ruled over peasants and had the pyramids built to preserve their memory.

Greece
A country in southeastern Europe. It is often considered the cradle of Western civilisation, since democracy and the principles of science, among other major ideas, emerged from here several thousand years ago.

India
A country in South Asia. Although home to large civilisations for thousands of years, it has only very recently become an industrialised nation. It now has one of the fastest growing economies in the world.

Japan
An island country in the Pacific Ocean in East Asia. Although isolated from the rest of the world from the 17th to the 19th century, it has since become one of the world's largest exporters and importers of products.

Middle Ages
The period in European history from the 5th to the 15th century, beginning with the fall of the Western Roman Empire. It is significant in part for the spread and dominance of Christianity throughout the countries of Europe, as well as for the millions of deaths caused by war, famine and plague.

Prehistoric
The mysterious, undocumented period of time between the emergence of the human species and the invention of writing methods that marked the beginning of recorded history.

Romanticism
An intellectual and artistic movement in late 18th and 19th century Europe that emphasised individualism, emotional experience and the awe-inspiring beauty of natural landscapes.

Roman Empire
An ancient civilisation centred in the city of Rome in the Mediterranean that conquered large parts of the globe, including areas of Europe, Africa and Asia.

Index

B
boots 16, 39, 43, 50

C
Cardin, Pierre 58, 77
Celtic 16–17, 66, 68, 79
Chanel, Coco 49, 53, 77
China 18–19, 66, 68, 79
Cleopatra 9–10
cloak 12, 14, 16, 27, 36
coat 5, 24, 32, 35, 37, 39, 41, 46, 51, 58, 62, 64
corset 29, 32, 36, 39, 45–47, 65–66

D
Dior, Christian 52–53, 76
dresses 9–10, 14, 24, 27–28, 30, 32–34, 36–40, 42, 45–55, 59–60, 62–64, 66, 75

E
Edwardian 40, 70, 74, 79
Egypt 8–11, 16, 67–68, 74, 79

F
fur 4–5, 16–17, 27, 44, 46, 51, 58

G
Gaultier, Jean-Paul 65, 76
gown 44–45, 50
Greece 12–14, 16, 37, 68, 79

H
hair 10–13, 15–16, 20–21, 23, 26–29, 30–31, 34–36, 38, 44, 48–49, 54–57, 59, 61, 63–65
handbag 35–36, 45, 51, 62–63, 66, 78
hat 12, 19, 24, 27, 30, 32, 36, 39, 41–45, 49, 50–51, 58, 64–65, 67, 72, 74
headscarf 54–55
heels 13, 30, 33, 41, 48, 53, 62, 66

I
India 22–23, 69, 79

J
jacket 34, 42–43, 49, 51–52, 56, 60, 62, 72
Jackson, Michael 63
Japan 20–21, 66–67, 69, 79
jeans 52, 57, 60, 62, 64, 66–67
jumpsuit 61

K
kimono 20–21, 46, 66

L
Lanvin, Jeanne 49

M
Madonna 65
Middle Ages 24–28, 69, 74, 79
Monroe, Marilyn 52–53

N
necklace 7, 47

P
pantaloons 36, 47
petticoat 29, 32–33, 39
Poiret, Paul 46

R
Romanticism 38–39, 70, 75, 79
Rome 9, 14–16, 68, 79

S
sandal 8, 10, 13, 15–16, 20, 63
sari 22
shirt 21, 23–24, 34, 44, 56, 61, 64
shoes 13, 15, 19–20, 24–25, 28, 30, 33, 36, 38, 50, 53–54, 60, 62, 64, 66, 78
shorts 51, 64
skirt 11, 16, 21–23, 29, 31–33, 36, 39, 41, 43, 50, 52, 54, 56 57, 59–60, 62–64
socks 16, 20, 53, 59, 63

T
tailcoat 36, 39, 44
trousers 16, 21, 23, 27, 34, 36, 38–39, 41, 44, 47, 50–51, 54, 56, 60–61
t-shirt 52, 57, 60, 62–64, 67
Twiggy 56–57

U
underwear 11, 27, 29, 47, 66

W
waistcoat 34, 54, 56
Westwood, Vivianne 60, 77–78
wig 8, 10, 31, 34–35